My name is Dina and this book is all about my Baba. He is the best dad in the whole wide world and the smartest. He never loses at Monopoly! Ever!

اسم من دینا است و این کتاب در باره بابای من است.
او بهترین و باهوشترین بابای دنیاست. بابا هیچوقت در مونوپولی نمیبازد، حتی یک بار.

My Baba is always there to guide me
so I feel brave trying new things.

بابای من همیشه در کنارم است و مرا تشویق
میکند که شجاع باشم و از انجام کارهای تازه
نترسم.

My Baba has a superpower. He can smack a watermelon and know if it is sweet and ripe. How cool is that?

بابا خیلی قوی است. میتواند با یک ضربه، هندوانه را بشکند تا ببیند شیرین و رسیده است یا نه. این عالی نیست؟!

My Baba is very serious when he works, but he is funny and playful when we are together.

با این که بابا وقت کار خیلی جدی است، اما وقت بازی با من، خیلی بازیگوش و با مزه است.

My Baba is very patient.
He can taarof with my uncle
for hours and not get tired.

بابای من خیلی حوصله و صبر
دارد. او میتواند ساعتها با عمو
تعارف کند و خسته نشود.

My Baba loves Rock & Roll, but
when he has time he plays tombak
and tar.

بابا موسیقی "راک اند رول" دوست
دارد اما گاهی که وقت میکند،
برای ما تار و تنبک هم مینوازد.

When I sit on my Baba's shoulders I feel like I can touch the clouds.

وقتی بابا من را روی شانه هایش میگذارد احساس میکنم میتوانم دستم را به ابرها برسانم.

My Baba works out,
but what keeps him
young are his afternoon
naps.

بابا ورزش میکند اما فکر
میکنم به خاطر خواب بعد
از ظهر، اینقدر قوی است.

My Baba loves picnics when he can make chicken Kabob for the whole family. Yum!

بابای من عاشق مهمانی در پارک است چون میتواند برای همه فامیل جوجه کباب بپزد، به به!

Earth

Moon

My Baba says science is the best way to explore the world. Learning about stars and planets with my Baba is always fun!

بابای من میگوید علم و دانش بهترین راه برای کشف دنیا است. برای همین وقتی با هم درباره آسمان و سیاره ها و ستاره ها یاد میگیریم، به من خیلی خوش میگذرد.

Jupider

Mars

Saturn

I know that even when I grow up I will always be my Baba's Fesgheli ...

من میدانم حتی وقتی بزرگ بشوم همیشه در چشم بابام همان فسقلی خودَش خواهم ماند ...

... and he will always be my
Baba Joon.

...و او هم همیشه همان بابا جونِ
من است.

When Shaadi can't find her rooster, Joojoo, she goes around asking her neighbors, the local baker, and the shepherd boy if they have seen her rooster friend. What Shaadi hears from them surprises her. She has taken care of Joojoo since he was just a little chick, and she hasn't realized that he has grown into a big and strong bird. Set in the charming village of Abyaneh, this story is about the power of love and friendship. Written for children ages 3 to 7 and their parents.

My Maman
بابان من
Anahita Tamaddon

Dina's
Ghormeh Sabzi
Stew
خورشت
فرمه‌سبزی دینا
Anahita Tamaddon

My Grandma
and Grandpa
مادربزرگ و پدربزرگ من
Anahita Tamaddon

My
Brother
برادر من
Anahita Tamaddon

The Meaning of Nowruz
معنای نوروز
Anahita Tamaddon

THE IMMIGRANT
GIRL'S GARDEN
ANAHITA TAMADDON

Anahita
Tamaddon
Mehregan
with My
Grandma
مهرگان با
مادربزرگم

Yalda Night
(in Persian & English)
Anahita Tamaddon

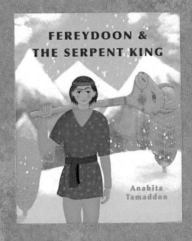

FEREYDOON &
THE SERPENT KING
Anahita
Tamaddon

THE PRINCESS
WARRIOR
Anahita
Tamaddon

Our Haft Sin
هفت‌سین ما

SORAYA'S
NOWRUZ
DANCE
(In English & Persian)
Anahita
Tamaddon

Yalda Night Celebration
جشن شب یلدا
Anahita Tamaddon

SHAADI &
JOOJOO
Anahita Tamaddon
شادی و
جوجو